CHARLIE

The Little Dog with COURAGE and SPUNK

Written By
WELDON CRISMAN

Illustrated By
NATHAN BIANCARDI

MANY**SEASONS**PRESS

Mesa, Arizona • 2023

FIRST EDITION

Charlie, the Little Dog with Courage and Spunk

Copyright © 2023 Weldon Crisman

MANY**SEASONS**PRESS

Published by Many Seasons Press
An imprint of Multimedia Publishing Project
PO Box 50553
Mesa, Arizona 85208-0028
480-939-9689 | MultimediaPublishingProject.com

Written by Weldon Crisman
Illustrated by Nathan Biancardi

Cover & book interior layout designed by Yolie Hernandez

Hardback ISBN: 978-1-956203-15-8
Paperback ISBN: 978-1-956203-16-5
E-Book ISBN: 978-1-956203-17-2

Library of Congress Control Number: 2023930003

MY SINCERE THANKS go out to Kimberly Crisman and Nikki Kingery. Without them, there would be no book "Capital Letters!" I want to thank all the family for being so supportive and just plain great!

I'll steal a quote from my great-grandson, Adrian, "I love them all to the moon and back!" Thanks, guys!

I want to thank the artist, Nathan Biancardi, a great artist and person to work with.

CHARLIE

THIS IS A STORY OF A LITTLE NEIGHBORHOOD dog with a lot of character and courage. Her life unfolded right before my eyes, or I might say adventure. How could I not write about one of God's little creatures, man's best friend. This is a story for people of all ages.

HI BOYS AND GIRLS. This is a story about a little dog with a lot of courage and spunk. It takes place from a few years ago until the present time. I know, not another dog story. This is a true story and one that's worth telling. I think all kids with a little imagination can kind of understand what the little animals are saying. That makes it all the better. We might stretch the truth just a little. Oh well, enough said. I'll let Charlie tell the story in his words. I'll start it out for you, Charlie.

Once upon a time, there… what…?

Wait a minute… hold on, Mr. C., that's the way fairy tales begin. This certainly is more of an adventure story.

Hi boys and girls. Let me introduce myself. My name is Charlie, and I'm a little Jack Russell. I'll bet your mom and dad know what kind of dog that is. I'm not very big. I only weigh about fifteen pounds, but I have an awful lot of energy. I just run around like crazy, having a good old time. I heard one lady say I was a little *hyper-dyper*—or over-excited. I don't know what that means, I hope it's good. I have another surprise for you. I'm a little girl dog. Fooled you. I'll bet you didn't guess that. Right? I think my master wanted a boy dog, but whatever came along was going to be Charlie. That's alright. It's a good name, and it seems like everyone can remember it.

I was getting a little older, about three years old by this time, and starting to remember things about myself. You know, all the good times. We kind of lived out in the country. There were farm fields right across the road and a big farm just down the road a ways. That road was sure busy. Cars were going by all the time. I can still hear my master yelling, *"Get back here, Charlie...stay away from that road. You are going to be in big trouble, missy."* I kind of got the message early on to stay away from danger. Most of all, I stayed out of trouble by minding my master. He was just looking out for me. I also had a big brother. I guess he was my brother. He was a German Sheppard. We played a lot together and had a lot of fun. I could run right underneath him. He played kind of rough sometimes. That was okay; if I got scared, I could run to him for protection. We sure had fun growing up together.

I will say, they watched me pretty close. I had a good home. They spoiled me a little, like all pets. My master was a recruiting sergeant in the Marine Corps, and when he had his uniform on, I felt pretty special. I spent a lot of time outdoors and, for the most part, confined to the backyard. They kept me on a pretty tight leash. That was ok, the backyard was big, and my master taught me to play ball. I liked that. What fun. He would throw the ball, and I would run like crazy and bring it back. That was good exercise. Everything was good, and I enjoyed my life. Sometimes I would bring the ball back, and he would say, *"Is that the best you can do, Charlie? Bring it over here, girl."* I would pick it back up and drop it by his feet. I wondered why he couldn't take that extra step, *"these humans."* Oh well, it was fun anyway, and he's the boss.

One day, there was an awful lot of excitement in the household. My master and his wife were talking. I heard him saying something about being transferred to California, a long way from here. I didn't know where that was, but they were really excited.

One thing for sure, that was the start of a lot of changes in my life. I didn't know it at the time. The days passed, and I heard them say the military would be sending a big moving van to move all of their belongings. It could happen any day now. He said his superiors told him that the dog was his responsibility and to make arrangements for the flight out west. They would either send for me or perhaps go with them on their flight. Sounded exciting. They decided something had to be done right away. I heard him say we

will have to pay for flying the dog to his destination. It was very expensive. His superiors told him only one dog would be allowed. Now, there was a big decision to make, *"what are we to do with Charlie?"*

Oh no, that didn't sound good. I knew they would come up with something so that I wouldn't get left behind. Wishful thinking. I learned quite soon that was exactly what was going to happen. He had to report for duty right away at his new location. Well, something had to be done immediately. They decided to ask their next-door neighbor if she would be interested in taking me. I didn't have much say so in this matter. They were trying to find me a good home. Their neighbor had a small son, and she thought maybe we would become playmates with each other. She agreed to take me. They were excited to get me and told them everything would work out fine. I was not near as happy as they seemed to be. It made me sad to see my family leave. They said goodbye to me, waved, and drove off. She told her son that his dad grew up on a farm in Iowa, and he always had a dog. He would like to have a dog running around again. This sounded like good news. Something positive. I decided to make the best of it. I couldn't change it. This was to be a new and very different chapter in my life.

I soon found out that being a pet with perks and being a dog are two different things. I was used to being an inside dog and a bit spoiled. I was now taking charge of my own life and becoming more independent. I had a nice bed in the garage, food, water, and a playmate; that's not too bad. I was not confined; what a change. This gave me a chance to investigate the neighborhood. I had never done that before. This will become quite an adventure for me. I didn't know where my master went, so I figured I'll just start looking.

I trotted down a couple houses from where I lived. My first stop was a lady that had some kind of shop in the back of the house, and I noticed a lot of women coming and going. They saw me and began saying, "What a cute little dog." They all had a good word for me. *"Isn't he nice?"* Everyone seemed so nice. I had never ventured out into the neighborhood before, so this was a good start.

I left there and went down a little further. There was a long street going down with a lot of houses on it and a short street off of it that ran right behind my house. A small subdivision. I could go right thru my backyard over to that street; what a shortcut. I didn't know it was there. I started out and went up and down the road. Most of the people seemed awfully nice. I would hear them saying, *"where did that little dog come from? He's new in the neighborhood"* There were some that yelled, *"go home, get out of here."* That was a clue to bypass those homes. It wasn't just the people; it was also the neighborhood dogs. Some of them didn't seem too friendly. I soon learned which homes I was welcome in. A lot of the people I visited had small children and didn't mind me being there. They soon realized that I loved to play ball. The whole family would take turns playing with me. More often than not, they would drop what they were doing and participate in my favorite pastime. They would finally get back to what they were doing, and I would move on to the next stop.

It wasn't long before everybody knew that my name was Charlie. I would hear them say, *"Hey, here's Charlie. He's come to visit. Oh, it's just Charlie."* They would start throwing the ball, and I would be right after it. It was great fun. The lady from the shop had told her customers my story, and they passed the word. Soon everyone knew about me and kind of felt sorry for me. Sure nice that they cared. Wow, everyone loves Charlie.

Well, time passes so fast, too fast for me. Summer rolled around after a beautiful spring. I like that season. Everything is coming back to life, including all the people. Everyone was back outside. We had some hot spells, and when I would stop by Mr. C's house, his wife would bring out a bowl of cold water and a little bowl of food for me. I sure enjoyed that because I probably just got done playing ball. It sure hit the spot. I wouldn't come around all the time, but I always knew I could get a bowl of fresh water when I showed up. I would play ball for a while, and then it was time to move on, but not before Mrs. C. came out with a treat. Some of the others would do the same thing. I couldn't eat all the treats, so I would bury them for later. This was not a good idea because when I dug them up, they had all disappeared. Not smart, no treat.

Sometimes I would visit my friends and was ready to play ball. Nope, they didn't have a ball. I started showing up with my own ball. The ball I would bring looked like somebody had thrown it away. It was better than nothing at all. We would play ball for a while, and when I would leave, I would leave with a better ball. I could hear them say, *"Charlie took the new ball, come back here, Charlie."* They really didn't care. Sooner or later, they would get it back. Time seemed to pass quickly. Everyone knew me by this time and looked forward to my little visits. That was kind of nice. Everyone loves Charlie. If I didn't show up for a while, they would start asking one another if anyone had seen me. It's a good feeling to know that they cared. Everyone always had a little time for me. Mr. C. would get off his lawn tractor when he spotted me, and we would play ball for a while.

The neighbor that lived across the street from Mr. C. had a large piece of a tree trunk on a stand. It was some kind of target, I'm guessing. I would watch, hiding from a distance. He must have been awful mad at it because he would throw knives and tomahawks at it. He seldom missed. He wore buckskins, and he had this cap with a long tail on it. I always waited until he put things away then I would stop by. I was careful so that I wasn't turned into a cap; besides, my tail is too short. I was told later by Mr. C. that it was a coonskin cap, whatever that is. I didn't want to trade places. Mr. C. said he was a frontiersman, and that is what he does. I do know that he and his wife liked me, and I liked them too. They were like Mr. C. and his wife. They always had time to play and make sure there was food and water handy.

In my travels around the neighborhood, I became pretty familiar with the people and their pets. I had noticed that this one house had a cute little dog like me. They didn't let him run loose. He was kind of like me growing up. They kept him on a leash. I would go and visit him. We got along well together. I heard Mr. C. say it was like Lady and the Tramp in reverse. I don't know if I like that. I guess my life was kind of routine. Time has a way of moving on. I would run the neighborhood by day and head for home when it started getting dark. The summers always went fast, and fall and winter would be here before you knew it. Old Jack Frost would be busy painting all the leaves in pretty colors.

I like fall, warm days, and chilly nights. Old man winter was close at hand. I never liked winter because I couldn't make my rounds and visit my friends. It was always too cold for anybody to be out, including me. I just couldn't wait until spring and summer rolled around and the warm weather to arrive. I could be back out and about visiting my friends and their pets. We were always glad to see one another again.

I am kind of getting ahead of my story. I had a major event in my life. I was confined a bit and didn't leave my house, and my visiting had come to a stop. Everyone knew I should be out making my rounds, especially because it was fall, my favorite time of the year. The next thing you know, my new owner was getting phone calls wanting to know if everything was okay or if I was sick or got in an accident. She told them that I had become a mother with a family of five little pups. That was a good reason no one had seen me. I was kept pretty busy. And, I stayed right there and watched over them. I had mentioned that fall was here and getting quite cool in the evenings. They had put a heat lamp over my little box, and it was nice and cozy. I heard Mr. C. say it was the same kind of lamp they used for baby chicks. I guess we had something in common with one another. It wasn't long; the word was out. Everybody wanted to see my little puppies. Mrs. C. came down with her granddaughter, some ladies from the shop, and others. Gosh, those little pups were the center of attention. It seemed like everyone was happy to see that I was alright and now knew why I hadn't been around. Everyone cared about me. How nice is that?

The weeks passed quickly, and the pups were growing fast. I had one little pup that got pushed aside by the others. Someone said, "That's the runt of the litter." I didn't care what they called her. That was the cutest little pup; the other pups were selfish and wouldn't let her eat. I could see right then that I was going to have trouble with my family of big bullies. A couple more weeks passed, and my master was concerned for the little one and said she couldn't keep them all. She thought the little one would starve, so she called Mrs. C. She came down and saw my family had all grown up. Mrs. C. fell in love with the little pup. She told my master, "I'll take that one." That sure made me happy. I knew she would have a good home. The first thing you know, her granddaughter wanted one. My master was going to keep one, and the lady at the shop wanted one. All of a sudden, my puppies were all gone. They had new homes. I had done my part and raised them until they were big enough to be on their own. I was happy. Winter was coming, and everything worked out rather well. They all had nice warm homes, but I really missed those little rascals.

I just had to get out and make my rounds before it got too cold. It seemed like everyone was glad to see me again. They were saying, *"Hey, Charlie's back, Charlie's coming, hi Charlie."* Wow, everyone loves Charlie. They are real friends.

My master and his family would take off on a trip every now and then. They had a little boy next door in charge of me until they returned. He didn't seem much bigger than me… Just kidding. But he wasn't too old and quite small. We hit it off right away. He would put a leash on me, and away we went. I didn't like the leash, but he was going to make sure that I stayed with him. He had friends down the street, further than I usually went. That was new territory, so it was exciting. He watched me for some time, and when we were really becoming good friends, his family moved away. That made me sad. Once again, someone left me. It wasn't too long until another family moved in. I thought maybe I would have a new babysitter or dog sitter. I figured I had better wait a few days for them to get settled in before going over. I waited for a couple days. I decided things had quieted down, and it was the right time to visit. I wandered over to their house and slipped into the backyard.

I didn't know they had a dog. There he was, a pit bull, I thought. I'll introduce myself and make friends. Well, before that thought ever left me, the dog was charging like a bullet. Wow, what a mistake. I couldn't even get my little legs moving before I was being shaken like an old rag. I was being bit all over, but I got a couple good licks in. I bit him on the nose. That made him madder. His owner came running out. He had heard all the racket that was going on. He grabbed his dog and put him in the house. The fight was over; lesson learned. Don't visit unless you're invited. I wish I had done that. I had introduced myself and found out, "Everyone does not love Charlie."

My master came running out, yelling and screaming. Everyone was in shock. It was a mess, not to mention me. The next thing I remember is we were in a car speeding to the dog hospital. I remember rushing into the doctor's office and then blank. They must have put me to sleep or something. When I woke up, I was in a cage. The doctor had put me back together. I was pretty bad. I had staples and stitches all over me. The doctor said I was lucky, and it could have been a lot worse. I didn't feel too lucky. I was sore all over and didn't feel too frisky. They had me confined after we got home so that I could recuperate. I was wishing I could visit my friends, but I really didn't feel like it. Anyway, I did need to get some rest. Everything hurt.

I didn't show up in the neighborhood for some time, and sure enough, the phone calls started coming into my master. Everyone was asking one another where Charlie was. *"Have you seen Charlie?"* No one had. So they went to the source and called my master. They wanted to know if Charlie had been sick or did something happen? She told them the story of my encounter with the pit bull. They were sorry for me and hoped I would recover quickly. Some time passed, and I finally felt like moving about. I decided to visit my friends. Everyone was glad to see me back. That made me feel good, and I already felt better. I didn't chase any balls, and I can't remember anyone wanting to play with me. They knew that I was still sore and healing up. That was nice of them. They all felt sorry for me. Well, time passed, and I began to feel like myself again. Once again, fall was upon us, and winter fast approaching. Days were nice and warm, but the nights getting cold. My master and his family decided to leave on a few days' vacation and asked the neighbor boy to watch after me. You know, food, water, and keep the garage door open for me. They would return in a few days. All was okay.

One day while making my visits and playing with every-body, I kind of lost track of time, and it was starting to get dark. The frontiersman told me to head for home. It was getting late. I listened to him. The weather was starting to get bad. Winds were blowing like crazy, getting cold, and I would be glad to get inside. I arrived at the garage, everything was locked up, and nobody was around. They had forgotten about me. Now it

The Ray
Family

was dark, and the weather getting worse. It was scary… what should I do? I know; I'll go back to Mr. C's house, you know, the person who started my story. I jumped against the storm door and barked. I thought they would hear me and let me in. No one came. The wind was making too much noise. I went across the street to the frontiersman's house. I did the same thing. I got no one's attention. I decided to curl up in the corner of his porch stoop. I thought maybe he would come out and spot me, and everything would be alright.

It was morning before he came out. He always went out to get the newspaper, and there I was. Boy, was I glad to see him. I was about frozen. I felt like an icicle. He took me inside and covered me up, and then I finally began to thaw out. Some food made me feel better. It was nice and warm. I soon fell fast asleep. Boy, he was not happy about me being left outside. He called my master, but they were still gone. I stayed put for a couple more days. Finally, they returned home. He was really mad when he called them on the phone. He told them they should have made sure I was being taken care of. Of course, they were sorry and thought everything was going alright. They were glad he was concerned and thanked him for coming to the rescue. A few weeks passed before they called the frontiersman, asking him if he minded them leaving Charlie with him while they were gone. It would just be for a couple days. A couple of days turned into a couple of weeks. He didn't mind me being there, but he was a little upset to be taken for granted. He thought a phone call asking if it would be okay would have been the thing to do. Well, things happen, and things come up unexpectedly. They were sorry. Seems like a pattern, but it didn't end there.

Sometime later, they called him again. They wanted to squeeze another vacation in before bad weather. Well, they were taken back a bit when he said *"yes,"* but and a big but, only on one condition: *"You can give Charlie to me, and I'll take care of her, or the answer is no. If Charlie is mine, I will take the responsibility for her well-being."* They told him that they would have to talk it over and think about it; it didn't take them long. They agreed. A paper was drawn up to make everything legal. It was signed, sealed, and I was delivered. I had a new master once again, not that I didn't already know them. Somehow, I didn't really mind.

The next thing you know, I was put into the car, and off we went to the pet store. They bought me a new leash and collar. I thought to myself, I wonder what they are going to do with those; after all, I'm not used to being on a leash. I kind of go where I want. Wrong. They had other ideas for Charlie.

The next stop was the dog hospital. He told the doctor to give me a complete checkup, shots, and all. Just fix Charlie up. Well, I didn't know anything was broken. The doctor gave me the shots, and they didn't feel good. He told him I had an ear infection and wanted him to leave me overnight. Sure enough, when I awoke, I was back in a cage. My ear hurt a bit, but he had called and said I could go home. He arrived, and the doctor gave him some ear medicine and told him that he was going to give Charlie a clean bill of health. If that was the case, I'm sure glad I wasn't sick. I guess whatever was broken was fixed, but I sure didn't feel that good. Home we went with orders to keep me down a few days. That wasn't too tall of an order because, once again, I wasn't too frisky. In a few days, I began feeling better, and they slipped my new collar on, hooked up the leash, and out we went. I wasn't used to the leash, but I guess he wanted to make sure I stayed with him.

It soon became a way of life, but I didn't mind at all. They would take me out, and I would see Mr. C. with his dogs outside. You remember that two of them were my puppies. I became a pet again after all those years. I had a nice home, a good warm bed, food, water, and best of all being spoiled and getting a lot of attention. The people would stop by when he took me out. They would tell him how happy they were that I was now part of his family. They all knew that I would be well cared for. I kind of miss not visiting all my friends like I used to, but I wouldn't trade the life I have now. You know everybody, this is a story with a happy ending. When it first started, I stopped Mr. C. when I told him that's how fairy tales begin.

Once upon a time, but I guess I was wrong because it really was a fairy tale with a happy ending.

THE END

NOTE TO READER: As the years passed by, I saw Charlie all the time. Her owners took Charlie out every day for her daily walks. She was a good little friend, and it was a good feeling to be part of her life. Charlie passed away on January 4, 2011.

Charlie is now in doggie heaven and, without a doubt, still chasing balls.

WELDON CRISMAN WAS BORN IN MILLER, INDIANA now part of Gary, Indiana, during the Depression days (1928). Soon after, his family moved to the country just across the road from his grandfather's farm. It was great growing up in the country. He got close to nature early on. He grew up fishing, hunting, trapping, and hiking. You name it, he's done it all. The author went to a country school with two classes in a room. Weldon always loved great subjects like History and Geography. He has always been an avid reader and is a big country music fan. His family didn't have all the luxuries we have today, but they always seemed to make out! He left school at 17 years old and joined the USMC during World War II and used the G.I Bill and went to college for a year. After a year, he decided to travel to see our great country! That's exactly what he did! It has been a great life and he thanks God every day!

www.ingramcontent.com/pod-product-compliance
Lightning Source LLC
Chambersburg PA
CBHW040905070726
47599CB00038B/2319